# HOUGHTON MIFFLIN
# Reading

# Animal
# Adventures

## HOUGHTON MIFFLIN

BOSTON

Printed in the U.S.A.

ISBN 0-618-16202-X

11 12 13 14 15 16 17 18 19-BS-07 06 05 04

Design, Art Management, and Page Production: Studio Goodwin Sturges

# Contents

# Duke's Gift

by Tricia Lee
illustrated by James G. Hale

Dad has a gift for Duke. It's this huge bone!

Duke checks left and right and
up and back.  He has not got a
safe place to hide his huge bone.

Duke hunts for the best place
to dig.  He digs up Dad's five
prize rose plants.

"No, Duke, no!" yells Dad.
"No more holes."

# Legs Gets His Lunch

by Chris Petersen

illustrated by Oren Sherman

It is wet. Legs hides in a small hole in a big log.

At last, the sun shines so Legs
pokes his nose out.  Legs spots a
plant where he can spin his web.

Legs can climb up and up.  He
will use soft silk to spin his web.

Legs hopes his huge web will catch a fat ant. Then Legs will get his lunch!

# The Nest

by Peri Jones
illustrated by Marcia Sewall

Jude found this nest in a big
plant by his home. Jude left it
and went to get Rose.

Rose bent down.
"This egg will hatch in no
time."

One morning, the egg had a
huge crack in it.
"It broke," yelled Jude.

Then Rose spoke, "The egg is fine. It's just hatching."

"It's so cute," said Jude. "It looks soft as silk."

# Seal Beach

by Carly Mackeen
illustrated by Marcia Sewall

Mom and I walk to the sea.
We take steep steps that lead to
the beach.

We see seals.  These seals
swim and dive.  We see them
eat fish and squid.

This seal pup wakes up from
its nap. It can't see its mother.

The seal pup keeps looking.
At last it sees its mother. She is
back to feed her pup!

# Pete and Peach

by Mack Duffy
illustrated by Anne-Marie Arcand

"Let's run and leap," yells
Pete the horse.
But Peach the cow just sits
in the green, green grass.

"See me leap this wall?"
yells Pete.

But Peach just sits in the
green, green grass.  She
smells a flower.

"See me leap this wide creek?"
yells Pete.

But Peach just sits in the green,
green grass. She smells a flower
with a bee in it!

"That is a fine leap, Peach!"
yells Pete.

# Gram's Huge Meal

by Edward Op
illustrated by Anna Herrick

Gram made a huge meal. She set it on a long, long table. Then she went to get Pops.

25

A white cow with black spots
leaned in.

"Pops will not eat these beans
and peas," she said. "This is
a fine feast."

A big black horse stuck his
neck in.

"Pops will not eat these green
grapes," he said. "This is a
real treat."

Pops and Gram came in.
"Yum!" said Pops. "Now this
meal is just right!"

# Rain Day

by Tina Mendosa
illustrated by Kay Chorao

Ducks play in this lake all day.
Ducks like it wet, so ducks like
the rain.

Frogs play in this pond all day.
Frogs like it wet, so frogs like
the rain.

This dog wags her tail and
jumps. Will she like it wet, too?
She may play in the rain.

We stamp our feet and splash.
We like it wet.  We like playing
in the rain.

# Cub's Long Day

by Mary Gold
illustrated by Anna Vojtech

This cub has big feet and a little tail. His home is a cave deep in the forest.

Each day the cub gets up to
run and play.  Then he rests.
When he wakes up, he is hungry!

He waits at the stream to
catch fish. He eats treats that
stain his face red.

Each evening, the cub finds
his way back home on the trail.

# Jay's Trip

by Jack Tanner
illustrated by Janet Montecalvo

Jay the snail has never seen
a bay. His home is near trees
and plants.

One fine day, Jay takes a nap
on this big red leaf. While Jay
sleeps, he sails a long way.

When Jay wakes up, he is at a
beach on a bay!  Kay gets Jay
and sets him in her gray pail.
   "This snail is far from his
home," she thinks.

That evening, Kay goes home.
Soon Jay is right at home, too!

# Word Lists

*Duke's Gift* (p. 5) accompanies *The Sleeping Pig.*

**DECODABLE WORDS**

## Target Skills
**Long *o:***
bone, holes, no, rose

**Long *u:***
Duke, Duke's, huge

**Final *ft, lk, nt:***
gift, left, hunts, plants

### Words Using Previously Taught Skills
back, best, checks, Dad, Dad's, dig, digs, got, has, hide, his, it's, place, prize, safe, this, up, yells

**HIGH-FREQUENCY WORDS**

**Previously Taught**
a, and, five, for, he, more, not, right, the, to

---

**Theme 6, Week 1**
*Legs Gets His Lunch* (p. 9) accompanies *The Sleeping Pig.*

**DECODABLE WORDS**

## Target Skills
**Long *o:***
hole, hopes, nose, pokes

**Long *u:***
huge, use

**Final *ft, lk, nt:***
soft, silk, ant, plant

### Words Using Previously Taught Skills
at, big, can, catch, fat, get, gets, hides, his, it, last, Legs, log, lunch, shines, spin, spots, sun, then, up, web, wet, will

## HIGH-FREQUENCY WORDS

**New**
climb, out

**Previously Taught**
a, and, he, in, is, small, so, the, to, where

---

### Theme 6, Week 1
*The Nest* (p. 13) accompanies *The Sleeping Pig.*

## DECODABLE WORDS

## Target Skills
**Long *o*:**
broke, home, no, Rose, spoke

**Long *u*:**
cute, huge, Jude

**Final *ft, lk, nt*:**
left, soft, silk, bent, plant, went

### Words Using Previously Taught Skills
as, big, crack, egg, fine, get, had, hatch, hatching, his, it, it's, just, nest, then, this, time, will, yelled

## HIGH-FREQUENCY WORDS

**New**
by, found, morning

**Previously Taught**
a, and, down, in, is, looks, one, said, so, the, to

**Seal Beach** (p. 17) accompanies *EEK! There's a Mouse in the House.*

**DECODABLE WORDS**

## Target Skills
**Long *e:***
these

**Vowel Pairs *ee, ea:***
feed, keeps, steep, beach, lead, sea, seal, seals

### Words Using Previously Taught Skills
at, back, can't, dive, fish, from, it, its, last, Mom, nap, pup, squid, steps, swim, take, that, them, this, up, wakes

**HIGH-FREQUENCY WORDS**

**Previously Taught**
and, eat, her, I, is, looking, mother, see, sees, she, the, to, walk, we

---

**Pete and Peach** (p. 21) accompanies *EEK! There's a Mouse in the House.*

**DECODABLE WORDS**

## Target Skills
**Long *e:***
Pete

**Vowel Pairs *ee, es:***
bee, creek, green, leap, Peach

### Words Using Previously Taught Skills
but, fine, grass, it, just, let's, run, sits, smells, that, this, wide, with, yells

**HIGH-FREQUENCY WORDS**

**New**
cow, horse, wall

**Previously Taught**
a, and, flower, in, is, me, see, she, the

43

## Theme 6, Week 2

### *Gram's Huge Meal* (p. 25) accompanies *EEK! There's a Mouse in the House.*

**DECODABLE WORDS**

## Target Skills

**Long *e:***
these

**Vowel Pairs *ee, ea:***
green, beans, feast, leaned, meal, peas, real, treat

### Words Using Previously Taught Skills
big, black, came, fine, get, Gram, Gram's, grapes, his, huge, it, just, made, neck, Pops, set, spots, stuck, then, this, went, white, will, with, yum

**HIGH-FREQUENCY WORDS**

**New**
cow, horse, now, table

**Previously Taught**
a, and, eat, he, in, is, long, not, on, right, said, she, to

---

## Theme 6, Week 3

### *Rain Day* (p. 29) accompanies *Red-Eyed Tree Frog.*

**DECODABLE WORDS**

## Target Skill

**Vowel Pairs *ai, ay:***
rain, tail, day, may

### Words Using Previously Taught Skills
dog, ducks, feet, frogs, it, lake, pond, splash, stamp, this, wags, wet, will

**HIGH-FREQUENCY WORDS**

**Previously Taught**
all, and, her, in, jumps, like, play, playing, she, so, our, the, too, we

44

Theme 6, Week 3

## *Cub's Long Day* (p. 33) accompanies *Red-Eyed Tree Frog.*

**DECODABLE WORDS**

## Target Skill
**Vowel Pairs *ai, ay:***
day, stain, tail, trail, waits, way

### Words Using Previously Taught Skills
at, back, big, catch, cave, cub, cub's, deep, each, face, feet, fish, gets, has, his, home, red, rests, run, stream, that, then, this, treats, up, wakes, when

**HIGH-FREQUENCY WORDS**

**New**
evening, forest, hungry

**Previously Taught**
a, and, eats, finds, he, in, is, little, long, on, play, the, to

---

Theme 6, Week 3

## *Jay's Trip* (p. 37) accompanies *Red-Eyed Tree Frog.*

**DECODABLE WORDS**

## Target Skill
**Vowel Pairs *ai, ay:***
day, pail, sails, snail, bay, gray, Jay, Jay's, Kay, way

### Words Using Previously Taught Skills
at, beach, big, fine, from, gets, has, him, his, home, leaf, nap, plants, red, seen, sets, sleeps, takes, that, thinks, this, trees, trip, up, wakes, when, while

**HIGH-FREQUENCY WORDS**

**New**
evening, far, goes, near, soon

**Previously Taught**
a, and, he, her, in, is, long, never, on, one, right, she, the, too

# HIGH-FREQUENCY WORDS TAUGHT TO DATE

| | | | | | | |
|---|---|---|---|---|---|---|
| a | does | girl | know | one | so | where |
| all | door | give | learn | other | some | who |
| also | down | go | light | our | soon | why |
| and | eat | goes | like | out | table | world |
| animal | evening | good | little | over | the | would |
| are | every | green | live | own | their | write |
| away | fall | grow | long | paper | there | you |
| been | family | have | look | people | these | your |
| bird | far | he | love | picture | they | |
| blue | father | hear | many | play | three | |
| brown | find | her | me | pull | through | |
| by | first | here | more | read | to | |
| call | five | hold | morning | right | today | |
| car | flower | horse | mother | room | too | |
| children | fly | house | my | said | try | |
| climb | for | how | near | see | two | |
| cold | forest | hungry | never | shall | upon | |
| color | found | hurt | not | she | walk | |
| come | four | I | now | shout | wall | |
| could | friend | in | of | show | was | |
| cow | full | is | on | sing | we | |
| do | funny | jump | once | small | what | |

*Decoding skills taught to date:* Consonants *m, s, t, c,* consonants *n, f, p,* short *a,* consonants *b, r, h, g,* short *i,* consonants *d, w, l, x,* short *o,* consonants *y, k, v,* short *e,* consonants *q, j, z,* short *u,* double final consonants, final consonants, plurals with *-s,* verb endings *-s, -ed, -ing,* possessives, consonant clusters with *r,* contractions with *-'s,* clusters with *l,* clusters with *s,* silent consonants *kn, wr, gn,* triple clusters, digraphs *sh, th, wh,* digraphs *ch, tch,* long *a* (CVC*e*), other consonant sounds soft *c* and *g,* final *nd, ng, nk,* long *i* (CVC*e*), contractions, long *o* (CV, CVC*e*), long *u* (CVC*e*), final *ft, lk, nt,* long *e* (CV, CVC*e*), vowel pairs *ee, ea,* vowel pairs *ai, ay*

46